Yamal : A golden boy who becomes a record-breaking star
Lessons for Kids

Copyright © Dzung Doan 2024. All rights reserved.

All rights reserved. No part of this publications may be reproduced, distributed, or transmitted in any form or by nay means, including photocopying, recording, or other electronic or mechanical methods, without the prior written permission of the publisher, except in the case of embodied in critical reviews and certain other noncommercial uses permited by copyrights law.

Information contained within this book is for educational purposes only. Although the author and publisher have made every effort to ensure that the information in this book was correct at press time, the author and publisher do not assume and hereby disclaim any liability to any party for any loss, damage, or disruption caused by errors or omissions, whether such errors or omissions result from negligence, accident, or any other cause.

ISBN : 9798300947453

First Edition : November 2024

This book is dedicated to

the dreamers, the doers, and the believers
to every child who sees the world as a field of endless possibilities,
and to the families and teams who lift them higher.

May you find inspiration in Lamine's journey and discover
that with passion, hard work, and support,
the impossible becomes achievable.

To the young stars of today and tomorrow
this is for you.

This is the story of Lamine Yamal, a boy who grew up to become one of soccer's brightest stars.

Lamine Yamal was born in 2007 in Spain, a country where soccer was loved by all. He grew up in a humble neighborhood with big dreams.

Lamine's family worked hard to provide for him, especially his father from Morocco and his mother from Equatorial Guinea. Even with the challenges they faced, they knew Lamine was special.

When Lamine was just a baby, his family won a raffle to meet the legendary Lionel Messi. While he was too young to understand, that moment sparked the beginning of his dreams.

One thing made Lamine's journey even more special: his father was not just a parent but also his personal coach. From a young age, his father guided him, teaching him how to dribble, pass, and play with heart. Lamine played with his friends every day on the streets, their laughter filling the neighborhood.

Lamine's family sacrificed much, including his mother moving to a nearby town to support his training. Their belief in him only grew stronger, even as obstacles came their way.

At seven, Lamine joined FC Barcelona's famous academy, La Masia. He was small, but his speed and skills dazzled everyone.

Yet, the journey wasn't easy. Despite being the smallest on the field, Lamine had to work twice as hard to prove himself. But he never gave up, turning his size into his strength.

At fifteen, Lamine's dream came true when he joined FC Barcelona's first team. But with this achievement came the pressure of the world watching his every move.

Handling this pressure was difficult for such a young player, but Lamine pushed through, proving his worth with every match. He knew that every challenge was a step toward his greatness.

Lamine's rise to success wasn't just about skill—it was about mental strength. Every time he felt the weight of expectations, he remembered his family's sacrifices and kept moving forward.

Lamine wasn't just talented as a scorer but also an excellent team player. He provided countless assists, making sure his teammates shone as well. His success was built not only on his own talent but also on the support of his team and teammates.

In 2024, Lamine achieved his greatest triumph to date. He was named Young Player of the Tournament in the UEFA European Championship, and he helped Spain lift the trophy. At just 17, he became the youngest player ever to win the Euro, an achievement that solidified his place in soccer history.

As he continues his journey, Lamine knows that no matter the obstacles, the love and support of his family, his teammates, and the lessons from his past, will guide him to even greater heights.

Lamine's story isn't just about soccer—it's about believing in yourself, no matter the odds. His journey from a humble neighborhood to the world stage shows that with hard work and heart, anything is possible.

Whatever your dream is, remember it's not just about talent. Surround yourself with people who believe in you, just like Lamine's family and team always stood by him. Their support helped him achieve his dreams.

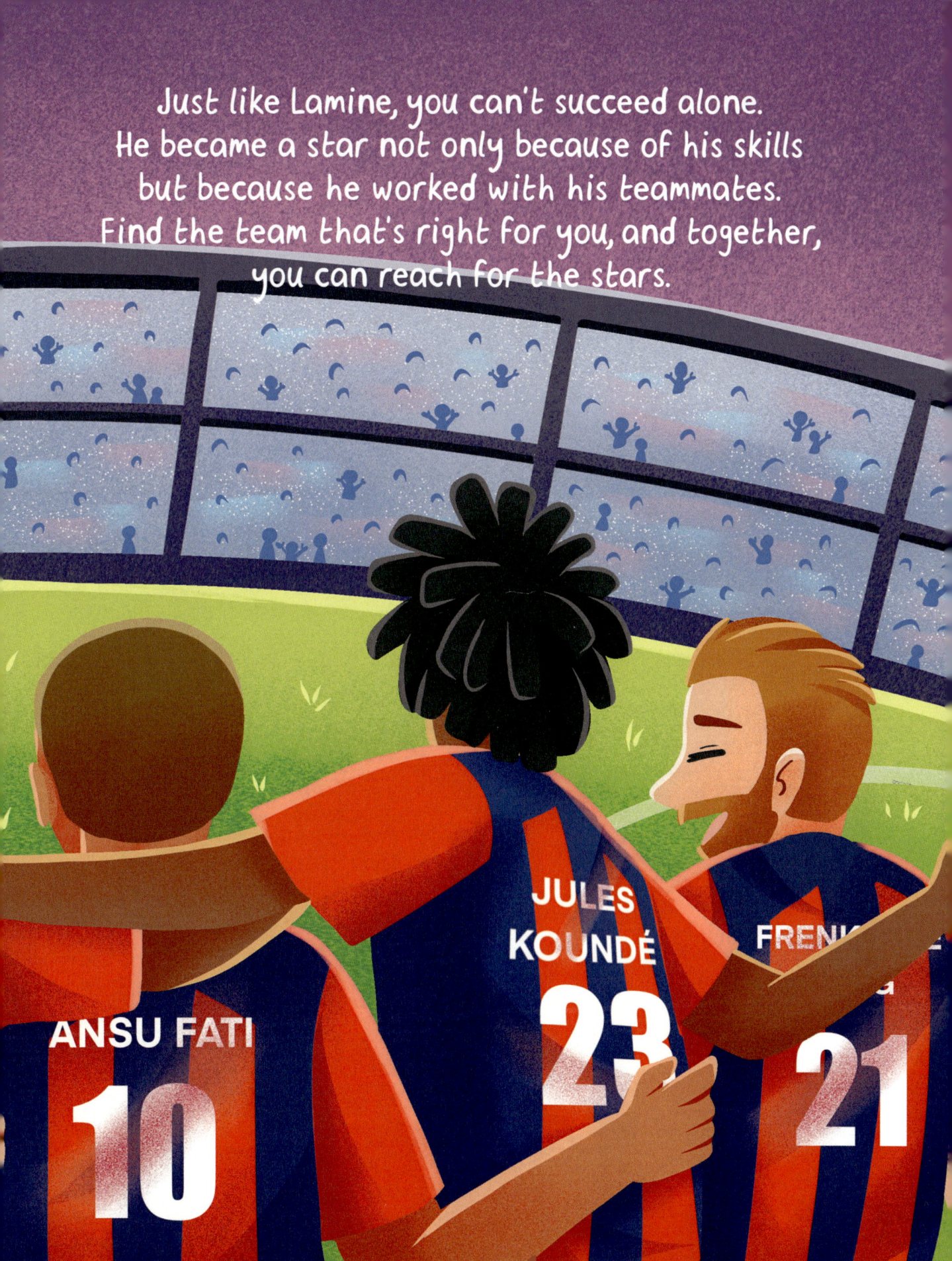

Thank you for reading my story!
Did you enjoy the book? If you liked it,
I'd love to hear your thoughts. Please take
a moment to leave a review on Amazon!
Your feedback means the world to me.

Made in the USA
Middletown, DE
19 November 2025